SCATTERED PEARLS

POEMS
that
TOUCH THE HEART
and
CHALLENGE THE LIFE

COLIN N PECKHAM

Scattered Pearls
available from the author
and
Faith Mission Bookshops:
2 Drum St., Gilmerton, Edinburgh, EH17 8QG, Scotland
5-7 Queen St., Belfast, N. Ireland.

First Edition
Dedicated

To

MY BELOVED MOTHER

"See you in the Morning"

Second Edition
Dedicated

To

MY BELOVED WIFE

Selfless servant; Practical wife; Soul-Mate,
Burdened intercessor, Anointed speaker & singer.
My Inspiration and Love!

Contents

Introduction

In the trysting place of intimate communion with God sacred beauties are unveiled that leave an indelible impression upon the soul.

Moments of God change a life.

This booklet is sent out with the prayer that these poems, which reflect such moments, will bring to the reader something of the atmosphere of eternity, something of the awe and adoration which an awareness of the Almighty produces.

May they inspire faith and obedience and result in deep and lasting blessing in heart and life.

Read - Ponder - Pray!

Cape Town   April, 1982
(Copyright : Colin N. Peckham 1982)

Second Edition

A few more poems have been added reflecting the warp and woof of life and, I trust, bringing further challenge and inspiration to the reader. Read slowly, carefully, thoughtfully, prayerfully. Let the words speak.

Some of the poems have been set to music and these songs are to be found in the *Songs of Victory*, the Faith Mission Song Book.* They are produced here with the tunes and numbers printed in bold type. Other tunes are suggested for some of the poems. These may be found in **Songs of Victory** (S.of V.), **Mission Praise** (M.P.) or in any other Hymnal or Song-book of the Church.

Further lists of tunes to which poems may be sung are to be found at the back of the book. Any poem written in CM may be sung to any other CM tune, or a poem written in LM metre may be sung to any other LM tune, and so on.

You can sing your way through the book!

May the Lord use this little book to thrill us, break us, bend us, inspire us and send us.

Colin Neil Peckham

1 Kilpunt Gdns., Broxburn, EH52 5AT Scotland
Email: DrC@Peckham.net
Web-site: www.revivals.org

Edinburgh   October, 2004

* Obtainable from Faith Mission Bookshops, UK.

Worship

Morning

"And he carried me away in the spirit to a great and high mountain, and showed me that great city, the holy Jerusalem, descending out of heaven from God, having the glory of God: and her light was like unto a stone most precious, even like a jasper stone, clear as crystal."   Rev. 21:10,11

The purest ray of virgin light
Unlocks the golden gates of heaven,
And issues forth in garments bright,
Illumines all that God has given.

Heav'n smiles upon the rising day
Through windows of the morning clear,
The curtains of the night away,
That locked the dawn in crumbling bier.

O holy virgin! Radiant morn,
Thy breath earth's fragrant raiments kiss
And all thy scattered pearls at dawn
Reflect the beams of heavenly bliss.

The music of the eager bird,
The joy of unspoilt innocence,
The ecstasy of heaven outpoured,
God's gracious holy reverence.

True Love throbs in creation's veins,
And joy flits round amongst the trees;
She sings her thrilling glad refrains,
And watches as the darkness flees.

But when that Morning gilds the skies,
And mountains quake earth's breadth and length,
The Sun of Righteousness shall rise,
And travel in His mighty strength.

Before the glory of that Morn
All other mornings fade away,
For Jesus shall the scene adorn,
The Lamb be crowned at Break of Day.

Creation strained His song to raise,
Its myriad tongues in faint employ,
But now the unchecked streams of praise
Fill all eternity with joy.

Eternal Morn! Thrice holy Day,
We worship in thy sacred light;
The King at last will come to stay,
His Presence banish all the night.

Adoration

Tune: **(8787D) Abbot's Leigh Songs of Victory 49**; Mission.Praise 187
or *All the Way my Saviour leads me;* S.ofV. 418, M.P.72
or Dim ond Jesu S.of V. 179 *Here is love vast as the Ocean*
or Ebenezer S.of V. 34, M.P.522 *O the deep, deep love of Jesus*

"And Thomas answered and said unto Him, my Lord and my God."
John 20:28

When the Lord shall come upon us,
And His glory we shall see,
Sense and know His power within us,
Feel His perfect liberty;
When the Lord our love possesses,
And His love pervades the whole,
How we easily surrender,
Oh, how Jesus fills the soul.

When He has our every portion
And His blood has touched the heart,
Cleansed, - we gaze and gaze upon Him,
Can it be! My Lord, my God!
How I love Him! Oh, I love Him!
How I clasp that matchless Name!
Jesus, Jesus, precious Jesus!
King of kings! To me He came.

Oh, I bend in adoration,
Jesus Thou dost flood my soul!
Jesus fills the very heavens,
He the Way, the Life, the Goal.
He the Saviour; His the glory!
Mortals worship! Angels! All!
Jesus, Jesus only Jesus!
While eternal ages roll!

Prostrate

Tune: (**SM** - 6686) Trentham S.ofV.570, M.P. 67 *Breathe on me, breath of God*
or Dennis S.ofV.184, M.P. 60 *Not all the blood of beasts*

"I was in the Spirit on the Lord's day, and heard behind me a great voice . . .
I turned to see the voice that spake with me. And being turned, I saw . . . one
like unto the Son of man . . . And when I saw Him, I fell at His feet as dead."
Rev. 1:10-17
"O come, let us worship and bow down: let us kneel before the Lord our
Maker." Ps 95:6

God comes, the Holy One,
Our great celestial Head,
His blazing glory streams upon
My soul so prostrated.

I bend, my lips are sealed,
God's presence fills the sky.
Almighty God to man revealed!
His grace has brought me nigh.

Prostrate before God's throne,
My vision focused all,
My love-filled heart unhindered flows,
Consumed my ravished soul.

With wonder, awe, I thrill,
The Christ I magnify,
His permeating Spirit fills
My life, to sanctify.

'Tis grace and mercy, love
Incomprehensible.
Fused and absorbed in Him above:
Joy inconceivable.

No boundary knows my soul,
Lost in this glorious bliss,
My throbbing, panting, melting whole
Receives God's tender kiss.

O God can man live on
In heaven's purest rays?
Our hope is in the riven Son.
Through Him alone we gaze.

Enough! O gracious Lord,
Thy name I but repeat,
My grateful life before Thee poured
Now bathes Thy bleeding feet.

Dwelling in His Presence

Tune: **(LM)** Deep Harmony S.ofV. 533, M.P. 620 *Sweet is the work* or Fulda SofV. 523, M.P. 728 *Lord Jesus Christ we seek Thy face* or Wilton S.ofV. 699a *O Thou who camest from above* or Holly S.ofV. 694 b *Lord speak to me.*

"He that dwelleth in the secret place of the most High shall abide under the shadow of the Almighty." Ps. 91:1

With Thee in secret, blessed Dove,
Transported to the heights above
Where in Thy glory I am lost
And worship with the heavenly host.

With Thee in secret, Holy One,
With Thee until my race is run,
The blood of Jesus is my plea,
Removes the guilt and cleanses me.

With Thee in secret, Love divine,
For I am bound by love first Thine,
United in Thy heart's embrace,
My soul exults in matchless grace.

With Thee in secret, gracious Lord,
By heaven's hosts, and me, adored,
Thy towering glory fades the sun,
Prostrate I all Thy beauties own.

With Thee is secret, Lord, my Love,
With Thee to sing Thy Name above,
And when Thou callest it will be,
But a brief step from earth to Thee.

Longings

Tune: (**LM**) as for previous poem plus Whitburn S.ofV. 694a, M.P.444
Lord speak to me

*"O God, thou art my God; early will I seek Thee: my soul thirsteth for Thee,
my flesh longeth for Thee in a dry and thirsty land, where no water is."*
Ps. 63:1

O Jesus Christ my sole desire,
Come burn with blazing holy fire,
Till all my dross is purged away,
And I stand in that shining ray.

Flow through my soul in draughts of love,
Lift skywards with Thee, holy Dove,
Lost, lost in Thee, Thou infinite,
Beyond earth's farthest gleams of light.

Far, far away from this world's plight,
God's radiant beauty meets my sight;
And Jesus, Jesus fills my soul,
Christ Jesus only is my goal.

My soul melts at Thy lovéd touch,
My Lover, God – no other such,
Exquisite to the single eye,
In Him I move, and live, and die.

Consecration

Tune: (**8787D**) S.ofV. 179 *Here is love, vast as the ocean*
or Hyfrydol S.ofV. 376, M.P. 226 *I will sing the wondrous story*
or *Blaenwern* S.o.fV 594 *LoveDivine*

"But what things were gain to me, those I counted loss for Christ. Yea
doubtless, and I count all things but loss for the excellency of the knowledge
of Christ Jesus my Lord; for Whom I have suffered the loss of all things and do
count them refuse, that I may win Christ."
Phil. 3:7-8

Hallelujah! I have found Him,
He is everything to me.
How He touches deepest heartstrings
In my inmost soul set free.

O, my precious, precious Saviour,
Take my heart, it is Thine own;
O my God, I love, I love Thee!
All my life is Thine alone!

Thine to do with as Thou pleasest,
Unreserved, abandoned, free, -
Yes entirely, wholly, fully,
Ever Thine alone to be!

Blessed Jesus, precious Saviour,
Thou who reignest in my soul,
Fill, possess, control and guide me
Till eternal ages roll.

Beholding

Tune: (**10 10 10 10**) Ellers S.ofV. 328, M.P. 584 *God made me for Himself*
or Eventide S.ofV. 417, M.P.4 *Abide with me*

*"But we all, with open face beholding as in a glass the glory of the
Lord, are changed into the same image from glory to glory, even as by
the Spirit of the Lord."*
2 Cor. 3:18

Be still my soul, thy God doth wait for thee,
He longs thy words of worshipping to hear,
His Presence sets thy heart at liberty
To soar to realms where He alone is near.

Be still my soul, the Spirit whispers still,
Cease from thy wand'rings – hear His blessed voice,
Come now and quieten all within until
His Presence is thy being's only choice.

Be still my soul – He comes! He comes to thee!
O blessed Master! Lord No words can trace
The preciousness of Jesus now to me,
I bend, I weep, I see His blessed face.

All else dissolves – my Lord alone is near!
I sink to nothing at His pierced feet . . .
His voice, His love, His presence – oh, so dear,
Prostrate, I but His wondrous Name repeat!

Worshipping

Tune: (**CM**) The Rowan Tree   S.ofV. 189b
or Westminster *My God how wonderful Thou art* S.ofV. 30, M.P. 468

"Worship the Lord in the beauty of holiness."
1 Chron. 16:29

O Jesus Christ, Thou living Lord,
My heart cries out for Thee;
My soul would seek Thee through Thy Word,
Thy glory I would see.

O Lord my heart with Love inspire,
To Thee alone I go,
My soul inflame with sacred fire,
Oh, set my heart aglow.

To catch a glimpse of Thy dear face
As all else disappears –
To bow within the trysting place
Thy glory see through tears.

Oh, lost in Thine enormity,
Entwined in Thy embrace;
Adoringly I know and see
Immensity of grace.

Waiting

Tune: (**CM**) The Rowan Tree S.ofV. 189b

"Truly my soul waiteth upon God: from Him cometh my salvation."
Ps. 62:1

O Holy Ghost, Thyself distil
Upon this waiting heart,
My all is yielded to Thy will
Lord, never to depart.

Thy gracious presence, O my God
This is my great desire,
Without this I am but a clod,
Yet with Thee, burn with fire.

O Spirit's wak'ning breath, blow on,
Descend, O God descend!
Revive Thy work! Exalt Thy Son!
O God, the heavens rend!

Beloved Jesus, Precious One,
My all is Thine for aye.
The glorious sight has but begun –
The breaking of the Day.

Conformed to His Image

Tune: (**CM**) Ballerma S.ofV. 372 *I waited for the Lord my God*
or Martyrdom S.ofV.556 *O for a closer walk with God*

*"For whom He did foreknow, He also did predestinate to be conformed
to the image of His Son."*
Rom. 8:29

Descend upon my soul, O God,
May I Your greatness know –
For You are all I long for Lord,
Oh touch me while I bow.

You are the King, the mighty King,
I own You Lord of all.
And yet You do to me impart
The grace to come and call.

Your song is in my heart, O Lord,
That angels cannot sing.
The song exalts the Lamb who died,
Makes earth and heaven ring.

For You I turn aside from all
That Your blest face would dim
I want alone to know Christ near
And be conformed to Him.

Hungering

Tune: (**CM**) St. Peter S.ofV. 97a, M.P.251 How sweet the Name
or Orlington S.ofV.438a *The Lord's my shepherd*

"Blessed are they which do hunger and thirst after righteousness:
for they shall be filled."
Matt. 5:6

O Jesus Christ, Thou blessed Lord,
Thy face we now would see,
Thy blessing cause to be outpoured
That we may worship Thee.

Yes here we come, great Seeking Heart,
And yield our all to Thee;
Our little all, how small a part
In view of Calvary.

Fill, fill the house with holy zeal,
Thy mighty power bestow,
Oh, melt our souls with Love so real,
And set our hearts aglow.

Descend, O boundless Love, descend,
With fire upon us fall,
Our prayers unite, the heavens rend,
And purify us all.

Then shall our mouths with laughter fill,
And great shall be our praise,
Our hearts shall bend to do Thy will
With gladness all our days.

O Lord in riches so divine,
My heart doth wide expand,
To hold not only Thee, but Thine,
And tribes in every land.

The Voice

"For this is he that was spoken of by the prophet Esaias, saying,
The voice of one crying in the wilderness, Prepare ye the way of the
Lord, make his paths straight."
Matt. 3:3

"I am a Voice," he cried.
A voice?
How strange that one should name him so.
A voice?
Yes, that is all –
A sound, a note, a strain –
No more.
Heard – then lost forever.
Resonance and accent –
Gone!
Ah, but aught remains;
'Tis what it brought.
The voice though lost
Hath clothed the thought –
That abides.
It plumbs the depths of opened soul,
Sinks and stays.
The Voice has been cut off
Long lost to human ear,
But in the midst it brought
The Word.
Lo –
He abides.

Christian Living

The Mystery of the Ages

Tune: (88 87) Green Point   S. of V. 390
or Old Yeavering M.P. 419 Like a mighty river flowing
or Ewhurst M.P. 257 I am not skilled to understand

"Christ in you the hope of glory." Col.1:27
"Christ liveth in me."   Gal.2:20

'Tis the mystery of the ages,
Hid from prophets, priests and sages,
God my seeking heart engages,
He stoops down to dwell in me!

Christ in you, the hope of glory,
Tell the world the wondrous story,
See Him come, His is the victory!
God stoops down to dwell in me!

God is for us, yes, but in us,
Naught but sin does He take from us,
Then His wondrous life He gives us,
God stoops down to dwell in me!

We partake of His own nature,
Thus to grow to His own stature,
While beholding Him in rapture,
God stoops down to dwell in me!

Guidance

Tune: (LM) Hamburg S. of V. 586 *I thirst, Thou wounded Lamb of God* or
Brookfield S.ofV. 499, M.P.346 *It is a thing most wonderful* or Woodworth S.ofV.
339, M.P. 396(i) *Just as I am*

"For this God is our God for ever and ever: He will be our guide
even unto death."
Ps. 48:14
"And thine ears shall hear a word behind thee, saying, this is the way, walk ye
in it, when ye turn to the right hand, and when ye turn to the left."
Is. 30:21

Renouncing all that others say
Of good or ill along the way;
Renouncing all the thoughts of those,
Who would their mind and will impose.

Renouncing indecisive plans
Of reason outside God's own hands;
Renouncing ingrained forms of thought
Where pain-filled battles have been fought.

Renouncing failure, fault and sin,
The grief, disaster found within;
Renounce external signs and tests
By which I sought to find sweet rest.

Renouncing all my rights and will,
My natural disposition still;
Renouncing every bit of me
O Lord, my Guide and Helper be.

Oh bring me quickly to the bar
And let Your judgement be the Star –
That guides through darkness to the Light
That shines upon the path at night.

And let me Lord no strange voice hear,
The precious Blood I plead – nor fear,
For Your protecting hand does shield
From fiery darts that demons wield.

Your plan for me show now, dear Lord,
The plan that heaven's vaults have stored,
Which when it touches mind and heart,
Will thrill and flame each little part.

Yes, He will tax the universe
To aid my search for His right course;
At last the Source of Light I'll see,
Your guiding Light directing me.

Trusting in the Storm

Tune: (LM) Arizona S.ofV.107b *Jesus Thy blood and righteousness* or Rimington
S.ofV.106b, M.P.171 *Jesus shall reign* (or Duke St.)

*"Thou art my hiding place; Thou shalt preserve me from trouble; Thou shalt
compass me about with songs of deliverance."*
Ps. 32:7

I never thought that I could bear
Such pain and sorrow, wretched care;
I never thought my life would be
So full of aching agony.

The storm bursts forth upon my soul,
The doubts and fears upon me roll,
The shattered hopes, the breaking heart,
My life, it seems, must tear apart.

But stealing from His heart above,
A whisper comes clothed in His love;
The words "Fear not" His heart unfold,
The words "Fear not" in burnished gold.

He stands between me and the foe,
I gaze till Christ alone I know;
Then rest in Him my hiding place,
And cling and trust His saving grace.

The devil's schemes to wreck, destroy,
Christ uses still in His employ,
And Satan's ruthless deeds but serve
To strengthen heart and mind and nerve.

Christ's presence in the storm's dull roar
Is worth ten thousand worlds and more,
I'll trust Him through the darkest night
Until my faith be turned to sight.

Suffering

Tune: (8787) All the Way   S.of V. 418, M.P.22 *All the way my Saviour leads me*
or St. Oswald M.P.338 *In the cross of Christ I glory*
or Stuttgart M.P.102 *Come, Thou long expected Jesus*

"For what glory is it, if, when ye be buffeted for your faults, ye take it
patiently? But if, when ye do well and suffer for it, ye take it patiently,
this is acceptable to God."
1 Pet. 2:20

Oh the blows that shock and stagger
As we seek to walk with Him;
Through the smart so unexpected,
Satan aims our light to dim.

Yes, the tides of spirit's anguish,
Ruthless sorrow, crushing, slow –
Do I turn me from this pathway?
All my being answers, 'No!'

In the depths, I learn such lessons!
Love burns fiercer than the flame.
Burning in and purifying,
Lifting up His precious Name.

In the crucible I find Him,
Here is fellowship divine,
Here the welding heart of suffering
Joins fore'er His soul to mine.

While the tears are falling freely,
Leaning hard upon His breast,
Songs in darkness rise within us,
Inexplicable His rest.

Oh the sweetest secrets whispered,
As I cling to Him alone,
Precious Jesus, precious Jesus,
Lost in Him – His very own.

Burn Out

Tune: (**CM**) Bays of Harris S of V. 550b.
or Glasgow S.ofV. 221 *Behold the mountain of the Lord*
or Sawley S.ofV 600 *Oh for a heart to praise my God*

"Why art thou cast down, O my soul? And why art thou disquieted within me?
Hope thou in God; for I shall yet praise Him, who is the health of my
countenance, and my God."
Ps 42:11

You've sailed in choppy seas, dear one,
The rocks have slit the bark,
The engine missed its certain beat,
Near gone its needed spark.

And oh, the traumas of these days
When hope itself seems lost;
When tears flow down the saddened face –
Your soul is wildly tossed.

Cling to Him in your deepest night
When prayer seems purposeless,
When Scripture seems a worthless book
And life is meaningless.

'Tis deep the vale and dark the night
Which your soul struggles through,
For few would understand your plight,
No sympathy is due.

But in the dark, and far ahead
There glimmers yet a light;
Keep moving on with dogged faith
And hold that flame in sight.

Despairing blackness yields to grey,
And hope will flicker too,
The panic moments shorter grow,
The sun come shining through.

For there are days both good and bad
As slowly you emerge,
Bad days grow less, and good the more,
As hope begins to surge.

He brings you out and leads you on,
'Tis oh, a shattering dream!
Hold fast to that dear pierced hand
As on His arm you lean.

Normality again will break,
And life once more make sense.
Relief will light the wounded face –
"Rise up, my love, go hence!"

The Heart Attack

Written to my wife and family after a heart attack in 1991 when I anticipated the worst. God, however, had other plans and I am grateful that He spared me to continue in His service.

"He shall call upon Me, and I will answer him: I will be with him in trouble."
Ps 91:15
"Fear not; I will help thee."
Is.41:13
"My times are in Thy hand."
Ps.31:15

Life is quickly slipping from me,
Through my hands its silver thread
Imperceptibly forsakes me
Leaves this sorrow in its stead.

So much still so unaccomplished.
Books to write and words to say,
Messages from heaven pouring
Through my faltering lips of clay.

But it's gone, the time has ended;
Oh, to speak His Word once more,
Oh, to preach with heaven's unction;
God Thyself upon me pour!

Days and nights of anguished labour,
Love-filled heart no more to beat,
Joy that swelled my soul with ardour,
All is ended at His feet.

O beloved, God will carry
You and yours through straits of time;
Trust Him in the lonely morrow,
He'll not fail, this Friend of mine.

He has seen me through life's problems
And He'll be so close to you,
And to our beloved children,
He'll not fail – He'll walk with you.

The Gardener

Written on the death of a young man who was killed in a motor accident.

"Ye sorrow not even as others which have no hope."
1 Thes. 4:13

The world is just a garden
Where many flowers grow,
And some are very precious,
For they with lustre glow.

Some tell us of our loved ones
Who now have gone before,
The fragrance of whose mem'ry
Within our hearts we store.

I lost just such a flower
'Twas plucked so young in life,
And ere the bloom had opened
The Gardener used his knife.

He plucked my precious Nicky –
We could not understand –
But trust in Him who loves us
To do as He has planned.

This flower has not faded
But lives and blooms all day,
Because right up in heaven
All night is done away.

There Jesus is the Gardener
He tends His flowers rare,
And everyone is happy
In His abounding care.

We'll meet again dear Nicky,
All tears be wiped away,
And Christ will be our answer
In that the perfect day.

Regrets

Tune: (**CM**) Jackson S.ofV. 251, M.P.323 *That man hath perfect blessedness*

"And Peter went out, and wept bitterly."
Luke 22:62

"The sacrifices of God are a broken spirit: a broken and a contrite heart,
O God, thou wilt not despise."
Ps. 51:17

I weep that I so blind could be
When Thou in love would guide,
What grief I must have brought to Thee
When I did not abide.

Had I but lent my ear to Thee
And leaned not to my mind,
Had I but seen as now I see,
This sorrow would not find.

Forgive O Lord, and draw me nigh;
Oh, clasp me to Thy breast,
That I might never from Thee fly,
But do Thy sweet behest.

My soul longs for conformity
To Thy blest will, O Lord,
My Conscious Intimacy be,
Nought else be my reward.

Farewell

– A family poem –
A father's tender farewell to his daughter before her wedding.
Christine was last-born and first married.

My darling little baby girl
With whispy hair so white,
We peered into your tiny cot
With love and great delight.

Our little "Toodles," "Milky Bar,"
Too fast, too fast you grow;
You little doll, you cheeky face;
Oh, how we loved you so!

You peddled at the standing bike
Your legs gave in, and we
Thought 'twas some strange paralysis –
You could not speak, you see.

And then you disappeared one day,
We feared that you were dead.
We scoured the bushes, searched the roads;
You hid just near the bed!

Remember "Boulders" and the beach?
Remember all the "braais"?
Remember long, long journeys too
Beneath the blue, blue skies?

Remember Onrus camping ground?
The Cape Peninsula?
Constantia house, the College and
Sweet Valley School so far?

And then the call to emigrate
Uprooted you from there,
And you grew roots in Scotland's soil
And Edinburgh fair.

The school of Flora Stevenson
Was where you learnt and played,
Then on to Mary Erskine High
Foundations there were laid.

Excelling as an actress, and
The gymnast of the year,
An academic prize you gained,
The prefect badge you wear

For hols to Europe we took off
And cooked beside the road!
And saw such wonders, had such joys,
And in our tents abode!

And then to Q.M.C. to learn
Of Therapy – and all;
The four-year Honours programme done
And now you're walking tall.

And then he came – as he must come –
With quiet eyes aglow;
You knew that he was just the man
You prayed for long ago.

Oh, how we bind him to our hearts
And welcome to your side
This fine young man who comes to us
To claim you as his bride.

Farewell my darling 'Bobsy' girl;
With all my throbbing heart
I'll love you all my given days
E'en though we dwell apart.

For Phil will care, and you are one
Complete as God decreed,
Together now to live for Him,
Fulfilled in Him indeed.

Our God will guide you both each day,
He step by step will lead,
Unite and use you in His will
As promises you plead.

We can but leave you in His hands
Rejoice with you, and pray
That God's rich blessings rest upon
You both from day to day.

All my love,
Dad.

The Resurrection

The Empty Tomb

"Jesus said unto her, I am the resurrection, and the life: he that believeth in Me, though he were dead, yet shall he live: And whosoever liveth and believeth in Me shall never die. Believest thou this?"
John 11:25,26

The poem ridicules the false theories which deny Christ's resurrection:

Verse 1.   *The Wrong Tomb Theory. The disciples went to the wrong tomb*
Verse 2.   *The Hallucination Theory. Mary had an hallucination when she saw Christ.*
Verse 3.   *The Swoon Theory. Jesus did not die but merely swooned and revived in the tomb.*
Verse 4.   *The Theft Theory. The soldiers claimed that the disciples stole His body.*

1.

Christ arose, but some reject it
'Nonsense' on their scornful tongue,
Erring women – so forgetful,
To the wrong tomb they had gone!

John and Peter too, mistaken,
To the wrong tomb quickly ran;
And the angel there to meet them
Made the same mistake as man.

Why did not the wise Sanhedrin
Go straight to the right tomb then?
Silence talk of resurrection,
Show the body to the men?

2.

Others say hallucinations
Were the order of the day,
Mary thought of resurrection
When she went alone to pray.

'Twas a great hallucination
For them all to see the same;
What an infamous deception!
All 500 made the claim!

Could the same hallucination
Come to folk so different?
At so many times and places,
Could they all this tale invent?

3.

Others say He did not die, but
Swooned and in the grave revived!
From the grave-clothes tight He struggled,
Weak and helpless, He survived!

Strength enormous He displayed then
Soundlessly He moved the stone,
Sixteen soldiers did not notice
He had ventured forth and gone!

Where, oh where could He have vanished?
Who protect His trickery?
He, the Truth, said He would die, so
Could He lie deceitfully?

4.

Soldiers say, 'they stole His body;'
If they slept, how did they know?!
Why take care to fold the graveclothes
If they had to grab and go?

Certain death to sleeping watchmen;
Would they all have slept in peace?
Why were not His own disciples
Forced to yield up the deceased?

Sorrow lay like lead upon them
How could they this action try?
Vile conspiracy was to them
Foreign, for they would not lie.

5.

If they only could produce it,
Place the body on a cart,
Wheel it through the streets in triumph,
Resurrection – blown apart!

In the world's extensive graveyards,
One Man left a gaping hole
To disprove the resurrection
That explain, oh faithless soul!

Oh the tomb is empty, Empty!
Hallelujah! He has gone!
Death is vanquished! He the Victor!
God's Almighty, Risen Son!

6.

And because they knew it, preached it,
They were beaten, tortured – died !
Who would give their lives defending
Falsehood, if they knew they lied?

It's the heart of the whole teaching,
If He rose not, faith is vain.
But He rose and lives within us!
Glory to His wondrous Name!

Now transformed, disciples preached Him;
Living Saviour! Loving Lord!
His the power and His the glory!
Risen and for'er adored!

Chorus:

Where is Jesus? The tomb is empty
Where is Jesus? Gone gone
Where is Jesus? He is risen, He is gone.

The Empty Tomb
(Abridged)

Tune: **(8787D)** Rosseau S.ofV. 573 *Church of God, beloved and chosen*
or Ode to Joy M.P.600 *Sing to God new songs of worship*
or Austria S.ofV.257, M.P.173 *Glorious things of Thee are spoken*

Him God raised up the third day, and shewed Him openly
Acts 10:40

Christ arose, but some reject it;
"Nonsense," on their scornful tongue,
Erring women – so forgetful,
To the wrong tomb they had gone!

John and Peter too, mistaken,
To the wrong tomb quickly ran,
And the angel there to meet them
Made the same mistake as man.

Soldiers say, "They stole His body."
If they slept, how did they know?
Why take time to fold the grave-clothes
If they had to grab and go?

Others say He did not die, but
Swooned and in the grave revived.
Sixteen soldiers did not notice
That He moved the stone aside.

If they only could produce it,
Place the body on a cart,
Wheel it through the streets in triumph,
Resurrection – blown apart!

In the world's extensive grave-yards
One Man left a gaping hole.
To disprove the resurrection
That explain, oh faithless soul!

Oh, the tomb is empty, Empty!
Hallelujah! He has gone!
Death is vanquished; He the Victor!
God's Almighty Risen Son!

It's the heart of the whole teaching
If He rose not faith is vain.
But He rose and lives within us!
Glory to His wondrous Name!

Holiness of Heart and Life

Seeking and Finding

*"For this purpose the Son of God was manifested that He might destroy
the works of the devil."*
1 John 3:8

*"Jesus Christ: who gave Himself for us, that He might redeem us from all
iniquity, and purify unto Himself a peculiar people, zealous of good works."*
Tit. 2:14

Long have I struggled with the burden of sin
How I have wept over wretchedness within,
Sin has invaded all my mind and soul,
I writhe in anguish in its vile control.

Chorus
Jesus my Saviour, cleanse my heart from sin,
Oh, how I long for purity within.
Sanctify wholly – and give me liberty,
O Jesus purge my soul,
I come to Thee.

When I would rise and live, O Lord for Thee,
Strangely I find rebellion lodged in me,
Then the battle rages – my whole soul is rent,
Who then will free me? Hope is well-nigh spent.

Oh, sin's corruption, filth and carnal pride!
Is its loathsome presence ever to abide?
Wilt Thou break sin's power? Wilt Thou set me free?
In desperation Lord, I come to Thee.

Lo, as I seek Thee, see the prayer prevails,
Lo, as I trust Thee, see the Blood avails,
Mountains of sin are cleansed for e'er away,
Jesus doth turn my night to glorious day.

Chorus (after last verse)
Jesus my Saviour cleanses from all sin,
His precious Blood – it makes me pure within.
Oh, Hallelujah, He gives me liberty,
Salvation full and free
I find in Thee.

Depravity

Tune: (LM) Rockingham S.ofV.195a, M.P.775 *When I survey*
Or Whitburn S.ofV.694a, M.P. 444 *Lord speak to me*

*"For the good that I would I do not: but the evil which I would not, that
I do. Now if I do that I would not, it is no more I that do it, but sin
that dwelleth in me . . . Oh wretched man that I am! Who shall deliver
me from the body of this death?"*
Rom. 7:19,20 & 24

"But where sin abounded, grace did much more abound."
Rom. 5:20

Invading sinful forces crush
And spoil, as through the world they rush;
Then can I hope to be made free
When this engulfs humanity?

Behold at times I lift my head,
And think to rise above sin's dread.
The tide unwholesome ebbs to flow!
And paralyzing death I know.

These reigning, carnal forces bind
My soul and heart and life and mind;
My agony is at its height,
Must it be thus both day and night?

O God, my tortured soul now still,
I long to do Thy perfect will,
But hindered by carnality,
I struggle in impotency.

My conscience stained, my will o'erpowered,
Affections and emotions soured,
Defiled my very thoughts and mind,
Within repulsive filth I find.

Oh, how the tyrant sin controls
The faculties of mind and soul!
How sinful sickness dissipates!
And filthiness makes desolate!

Oh, where is there escape for me?
Where can I find His purity?
How can my soul be filled with God?
Be kept alone for His abode?

Is there no rest; Is there no joy?
My all to use in His employ?
Canst Thou not cleanse and set me free?
O God, my God, deliver me!

Now lo! What says the Word to me?
What! Can I grasp it and be free?
"Where sin abounds, grace does the more!"
Sin flees as I this grace implore!

God's Word! Enough His plan to trace,
Christ's Blood! The riches of His grace,
The Holy Ghost then brings to me
The truth, that trusting, sets me free!

And every passage sin possessed,
And all its vileness in my breast,
As faith leaps to this mighty word,
Sin yields to its all-conquering Lord!

Sin's awesome power does Christ divest,
In Him at last I find sweet rest,
Grace channels in His purity,
And in Him I find liberty.

'But
where sin
abounded,
....

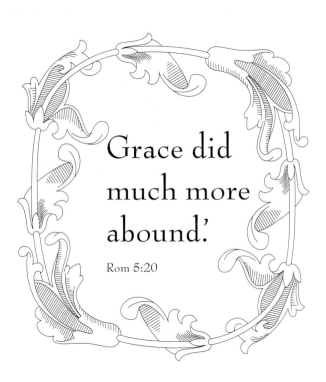

Grace did
much more
abound.'

Rom 5:20

Claiming Promised Purity

Tune: (DLM) Tokai S.ofV. 571 or S.ofV. 423 He leadeth me
or St. Clement S.ofV.657b, M.P.641 *The day Thou gavest Lord is ended*

*"But as He which hath called you is holy, so be ye holy in all manner of
conversation; because it is written, Be ye holy; for I am holy."*
1 Peter 1:15,16
"This is the will of God, even your sanctification."
1 Thes.4:3
"And the very God of peace sanctify you wholly."
1 Thes.5:23

Before Your holiness I bow,
O Jesus come and cleanse me now,
Oh come, and take away my sin,
And purify me deep within.
I grieve, I grieve, this dreadful state,
The evil hid within, I hate,
The good I would, but cannot do,
I'm left the evil to pursue.

Defiled my very thoughts and mind,
Within repulsive sin I find.
How sinful sickness dissipates,
And filthiness makes desolate!
Oh, where is there escape for me?
Where can I find His purity?
Oh, come Lord Jesus, set me free,
And by Your Blood deliver me!

Your Word is surely ever true,
And what You promise You will do,
So when You claim to purify
This must be true; God cannot lie.
I come then, Jesus, and I stake
My all upon the Word I take.
It is enough! God's Word to me
Will hold throughout eternity.

I claim in faith, the prayer prevails,
And as I trust the Blood avails,
Sin's power is broken, and I know
 My heart is cleansed as white as snow;
The Spirit speaks the Word to me
Which gives me glorious liberty
And all my heart is Yours to fill,
To live forever in Your will.

Exposed

Tune: (**86886**) Newcastle S.ofV.547 *Eternal Light*
or St. Margaret M.P. 515 *Oh love that will not let me go*

*"All things are naked and opened unto the eyes of Him with
whom we have to do."*
Heb. 4:13

And do you writhe in outraged pride,
O soul crushed by remorse?
To think that such a thing could hide
Within, where Blood had been applied,
And find not there recourse!

The deed is done, the word is said,
And shame brings agony,
You have been seen of men and read,
And their appraisal is your dread,
The carnal self they see.

Beware lest you side-step the Cross
In this your crisis hour,
Excuse so subtly selfish dross,
And gain your life when death seems loss,
And miss His path, His power.

Pure freedom comes when that big "I"
Determinedly is brought
By faith to Calvary to die,
No more in hidden forms to lie,
Deliverance then is wrought.

Then will you come and bring your load
Of sullen, wounded pride?
No other way, no other road,
To perfect rest and joy in God,
Than with Him crucified.

Cleansing

Tune: **(86886) S. of V. 584** or Newcastle S.ofV.547 *Eternal Light*
or St. Margaret M.P.515 *Oh Love that will not let me go*
or Repton M.P. 111 *Dear Lord and Father of mankind*

"Blot out all mine iniquities. Create I me a clean heart , O God"
Ps. 51:9&10

I come, my God, for cleansing, free,
From sin's defiling stains,
I see, O God, I weep to see
The sinfulness corrupting me
Which in my heart remains.

I hate my envy and my pride,
My failure and my sin.
To think that all these things could hide
Within, where blood had been applied,
And stay concealed therein.

I come, Lord Jesus, hear my cry,
Oh, cleanse my heart today.
I come to Calvary to die,
And with Your death identify,
This is the only way.

I come, I trust, and now I see
The power of Jesus' blood;
Grace channels in His purity,
And in Him I find liberty
And rest and joy in God.

Believing

Tune: (LM) Ombersley S.ofV.686, M.P.250 *How shall they hear?*
or Hereford S.ofV.699b *O Thou who camest from above*

*"Now faith is the substance of things hoped for, the evidence
of things not seen."*
Heb. 11:1

"For we which have believed do enter into rest."
Heb. 4:3

In absolute sincerity,
I sought for peace and purity,
I struggled to believe the Word,
And yet no peace would this afford.

Long have I fought with sinfulness,
With burdened prayers I longed for rest,
But now my struggles I give o'er,
Come sanctify and make me pure.

Before Your holiness I bend,
My soul from sin, O God, now rend,
Oh come and purge with Fire divine,
Come reign within this heart of mine.

Now Lord I kneel down at Your feet,
Oh come and do the work complete;
I trust at last Your cleansing power,
And dare believe this very hour.

Now

Tune: (7777D) Noordhoek S.of V. 633 or Everlasting Love S.ofV.506, M.P. 452
I am His (Loved with everlasting love) or Hollingside S.ofV.522a *Jesus Lover of my soul*

"Behold, now is the accepted time; behold now is the day of salvation."
2 Cor. 6:2

"Again he sets a certain day, "Today", saying through David so long afterward, in the words already quoted, "Today, when you hear his voice, do not harden your hearts."
Heb. 4:7 (R.S.V)

"There remaineth therefore a rest to the people of God."
Heb. 4:9

Never later than this day –
Now, my God, Thy power display.
Now, oh cleanse by Jesus blood,
Set me free to live for God.

Vain the worldling's fleeting joys,
Vain his pomp, his power, his poise.
Lord I come again to Thee,
Christ my present Saviour be.

Now my longing soul, Lord fill,
Now restore to do Thy will,
Desperate, Lord, I fall on Thee,
Now my God, deliver me.

Perish every vain desire,
Burn with pure, celestial fire,
Holy Ghost Thy promise prove,
Fill me now with perfect love.

On Thy Word my stand I take,
Thou dost cleanse for Jesus sake!
Thou the mighty work must do,
To Thy promises be true.

Now the blood doth sanctify,
Now with Christ I gladly die,
Now the Holy Ghost doth purge,
Now through all, His life doth surge.

Lord, the wonder of this hour,
God has come in mighty power,
Sinful fetters broken lie,
God by grace hath brought me nigh.

What redemption Lord I find!
God possessing heart and mind.
Thou, O Lord, doth set me free,
All my life I yield to Thee.

Liberty

Tune: (8888) Hamburg S.ofV.586 *I thirst, Thou wounded Lamb of God*
(Also 7777D as in "Now")

"Having therefore these promises, dearly beloved let us cleanse ourselves from all filthiness of the flesh and spirit, perfecting holiness in the fear of God."
2 Cor. 7:1

Sin's pollution wracked my soul,
Hidden deep within my breast,
How I longed to be made whole,
Cleansed and healed, and given rest.

Ah, the fight with rebel powers,
Oh to be at liberty!
Struggling in the early hours,
Seeking God to be set free.

Great the Light when first it broke,
Streamed the glory deep within,
Wondrous day – to me He spoke:
Jesus' Blood sets free from sin.

Had I not believed this fact?
Yes, but never till this hour
Did I see 'twas God's own act,
God's own sanctifying power.

God in Christ has set me free
Through the sacrifice divine,
And His blood releases me
Into fellowship sublime.

The Blood

Tune: (**8888**) Woodworth S.ofV.339, M.P.396(i) *Just as I am*
or Hamburg S.ofV.586 *I thirst, Thou wounded Lamb of God*

"Redeemed . . . with the precious blood of Christ."
1 Pet. 1:18,19

"For it is the blood that maketh atonement for the soul."
Lev. 17:11

"The blood of Jesus Christ His Son cleanseth us from all sin."
1 John 1:7

*"These are they which . . . have washed their robes and made them
white in the blood of the Lamb."*
Rev. 7:14

The law exposes all my sins,
Pronounces guilty and condemns,
But Jesus Christ has died for me,
His Blood – this my only plea.

Forgiven, yet I sometimes sigh,
And oft am torn in anguish by
The loathsome sense of inward sin,
And yearn for cleansing deep within.

Ah, life is in the Blood we know –
The Blood that washes white as snow –
I trust! The cleansing now takes place!
Abundant life does sin replace.

A thousand faults and failings I,
The perfect law demands I die,
But Lord – the Blood, the Blood speaks free,
The precious Blood it shelters me!

Beneath this flow I walk in white,
And step with Him in purest light,
And gratefully behold the Tree –
My wonder still – Christ died for me.

Identification

Tune: (CM) St. Columba S.ofV.247 *Come Holy Ghost our hearts inspire*
or Salzburg S.ofV.435 *O God of Bethel*
or Creator God S.ofV.464, M.P.583 *Safe in the shadow of the Lord*

"I am crucified with Christ: nevertheless I live; yet not I, but Christ liveth in me."
Gal. 2:20

"He that is dead is freed from sin."
Rom. 6:7

In twain is cleft eternity.
God looks not on His Son,
The rays which stream on Calvary
Sin claims them every one.

The bitter cup, He empties all,
Alone the God-man cries
"Forsaken," hear that sad word roll,
The sinner's death He dies.

The mystery deeps; in holy tryst
The putrid fumes of sin,
As I hold fast the dying Christ,
Extinguishéd in Him.

The inner conflict, anger, pride,
Sin's iron rule is broke.
Unclean, rebellious, I despaired,
He slays all at a stroke.

He dies! I die! Is this God's plan?
Is this enough for me?
The wonder of God's word to man:
He that is dead is free!

The doorway of deliverance death,
With Him identified.
His victor's life my every breath,
He lives, the Crucified.

Revival

Send the Floodtides

Tune: **(8787) S. of V. 665** or S.ofV.605a, M.P.948 All for Jesus
or Cross of Jesus S.of V. 293, M.P. 607 *There's a wideness in God's mercy*
or St. Andreew S. of V. 693a, or St. Oswald S.of V. 693b *Jesus calls us*

*"When the Lord turned again the captivity of Zion, we were like them that
dream. Then was our mouth filled with laughter, and our tongue with singing:
then said they among the heathen, The Lord hath done great things for them.
The Lord hath done great things for us; whereof we are glad."*
Ps. 126:1-3

Send the floodtides of Your blessing!
Pour exhaustless draughts of grace;
In the spate of heavenly glory
O my God, spare me a place.

Come around us, o'er us, on us,
Fill our souls with holy fire,
Come in glory – stand among us!
O my soul, to God aspire!

Cleanse! O mighty floodtide – cleanse me
Purer than the driven snow!
Oh the precious blood does reach me,
His blest cleansing now I know!

God is here in matchless splendour,
Gone the glory of earth's sun,
Blinded by the vision glorious,
Lord in me, Your will be done.

Hallelujah! Glory! Glory!
God in majesty just sweeps,
Gushing forth in mighty torrents,
O'er the land His power now leaps.

O Great Victor – ride in Triumph!
Blood-bought riches You must claim,
On till we with hosts of glory
Swell fore'er Your mighty Name!

Service

But If I Die ...

Tune: (10 10 10 10) Morecambe S.ofV.555, M.P.470 *My goal is God Himself*
or Eventide S.ofV.417, M.P.4 *Abide with me*

*"Verily, verily, I say unto you, Except a corn of wheat fall into the ground and
die, it abideth alone: but if it die, it bringeth forth much fruit!"*
John 12:24

'Twas black, the midday darkness on that day,
The cup of sin was filléd to its brim,
The ghastly cup that quenched each heavenly ray,
And called eternal wrath to fall on Him.

Oh, ne'er had Sorrow's heart asunder torn!
Oh, never had a Price like this been paid!
My God, He's dead! O Earth! O Heaven! Mourn!
Behold the mighty Sacrifice is made!

The Corn of Wheat lay buried, buried deep
Within the bowels of earth – alone, alone!
The grave the Corn of Wheat shall safely keep!
The sepulchre they locked with mighty stone!

'Tis not the end! 'Tis not the end – the grave!
'Tis but the doorway unto life, to die!
Behold the empty Tomb! He rose to save!
And now the Corn of Wheat can multiply.

The dying Corn of Wheat has given root –
Behold, the swaying harvest lives in Him,
Red life has burgeoned forth amazing fruit,
That swells redemption's never-dying hymn!

O Corn of Wheat, is this the only way?
Then to the Cross, the place of death for me,
To self in all its hidden forms; and yea,
The sheaves which You will garner, we shall see.

Wrestling in Prayer

Tune: (8888) Hamburg S.ofV.586 *I thirst thou wounded Lamb of God*

"And Moses returned unto the Lord, and said, Oh, this people have sinned a
great sin; . . . Yet now, if Thou wilt forgive their sin -; and if not, blot me, I pray
Thee, out of Thy book which Thou hast written."
Ex. 32:31,32

"For I could wish that myself were accursed from Christ for my brethren, my
kinsmen according to the flesh."
Rom. 9:3

"Rachel . . . said unto Jacob, "Give me children or I die."
Gen 30:1

Barren altars! What reproach!
Empty cribs! The church forlorn.
Hear we ne'er God's grand approach?
Blessed cry of babes new-born?

Havoc wrought midst Zion's sons,
Dimly burns the feeble flame.
Few the faithful burdened ones,
Vision, passion – but a name!

Bloodless prayers can never bless,
God forgive! Oft these are mine.
Give, O Christ, Thy brokenness,
Pain-filled fellowship divine.

Christ dwells in the broken heart,
This enshrines Gethsemane,
Oh, dear Lord, give me this part,
Sacrificial ministry.

Servants of His passion we,
Dazed and aching for the lost,
Marked the sighing forehead see,
One with Christ at life-blood cost.

Supplicate in bloody sweat,
Intercede in agony.
Plead for souls with faces wet,
Passion learned at Calvary.

Souls! My heart breaks with the cry,
What counts else! What matters more!
Give me souls or else I die!
Violence storms at heaven's door.

Sobbing in the secret place,
Broken-hearted anguish know,
Children will be born in grace,
God's transforming blessing flow.

Earnest spirit's fervency,
Flaming breath ascends, avails,
Prayer transcends vocab'lary,
Spirit unctioned prayer prevails.

Heav'ns shall rend and mountains flow,
Fiends of hell in terror flee,
Christ shall reign above, below!
His the glorious Victory!

First the Kingdom

Tune: (11 10 11 10) Lord of the Years S.ofV.524, M.P.428 or So send I you S.ofV. 706 or Finlandia S.ofV.468, M.P.98 *We rest on Thee*

"But seek ye first the kingdom of God, and His righteousness; and all these things shall be added unto you."
Matt. 6:33

"Jehovah-jireh" (The Lord will provide).
Gen. 22:14

They left their earthly ties and warmth of friendship,
Security of wealth and prospects grand,
A call compelled them, and beneath His Lordship,
They yielded all and grasped His guiding hand.

And through the years the message burned within them,
And o'er and o'er they preached the blessed Word,
They gave their lives, and prayed, and wept, and laboured,
And conquered with the Spirit's mighty sword.

This God who bid them, "Seek ye first the kingdom,"
To whom they yielded life and earthly store,
Had promised to support and to sustain them,
On Him their gaze was fixed as ne'er before.

And did He fail them having pledged His promise?
Did He forsake them, blushing in their shame?
His presence filled them with such joy and gladness,
Jehovah-jireh is His blessed Name!

This God to all His promises is faithful,
Touched hearts and through them all their need supplied,
Till they, amazed and humbled, glad and grateful,
Just worshipped Him; on whom they had relied.

To Him the glory, His the praise forever,
Whate'er He gave, they but returned again,
Themselves afresh they placed upon the altar,
Their gift of joy to praise His matchless Name.

My Hand Upon The Plough

Tune: (CM) St. Agnes, Durham S.ofV.503 *Jesus the very thought of Thee*
or Lloyd S.ofV.97c *How sweet the Name of Jesus sounds*

*"And Jesus said unto him, No man, having put his hand to the plough, and
looking back, is fit for the kingdom of God."*
Luke 9:62

My hand is on the plough, O Lord,
I hear Your solemn call,
Your separating Spirit's sword
Has claimed and conquered all.

I gladly yield to Your blest will,
And know Your hand will guide
While my fixed gaze beholds You still,
Nor turns from You aside.

Ah yes, the blazing sun will burn,
The field will be so rough,
The soil be caked and hard to turn,
My body cry, "Enough."

The time may come when I shall hear
Some voice that calls aside,
To turn from this which now is clear,
In comfort to abide.

But, O my God, Your highest choice!
Your will! – my constant cry.
For I would have no other Voice
To guide me till I die.

To souls in need I now must go,
The gospel they must hear,
To weep, to pray, to bend, to sow –
The peerless pathway here!

Empower with holy strength, O God,
That nought too hard may be;
That I shall plough with You the sod,
Your garnered harvest see.

Listening

Tune: (**CM**) Rachel S.ofV. 97b *How sweet the name* or Abney S.ofV 170. *Alas and did my Saviour bleed* or Abridge S.ofV.411, M.P.31 *O Jesus Christ grow Thou in me.*

I speak to the world those things which I have heard of Him.
As my Father hath taught me, I speak these things. And He that sent me is with
me. I speak that which I have seen with My Father
John 8:26,28,29, 38.

I speak the things I hear from Him,
Not just the words I read;
Whilst those enhance my intellect
My spirit I must feed.

To listen is my chiefest aim,
To catch the heavenly sound,
Hush, oh my soul, to hear the voice
That in His word is found.

Oh, speak to me, my blessed Lord,
All inner voices still,
I wait in silence at Your feet
To know Your word and will.

How blessed is that spoken word,
The word of God to me,
I bend, I break, and worship here
In deep humility

This feeds my soul – I hear from God,
What joy wells up in me,
My heart now finds its home in Him
Who sets my spirit free.

How precious is this trysting place
Of God's communion sweet.
The secrets He imparts to me
Make all my joy complete.

His are the words I now can speak,
His words writ deep in me.
They freely flow from burning lips,
And from a heart set free.

This Grace of Giving ...

Tune: (**CM**) Effingham S.ofV.62 *His Name for ever shall endure*

" . . *to test the sincerity of your love.*"
2 Cor. 8:7,8 (N.I.V)

O friend, how can you sit at ease
And hear the dying cry?
While death and hell their millions seize,
Your eyes, my friend, are dry!

The things to which you firmly cling
Are victims of decay;
No matter how much joy they bring
They soon must pass away.

Does selfish spending illustrate
Your egotistic style?
And treasures but accumulate
While you so proudly smile?

The pleasant ways which riches give
Have numbed your senses quite,
You cannot see that these who live,
Are dead in hell's dark night.

Do hoarded riches your hands stain
With blood of those who die?
And do you dare His love to claim,
Who pleads with heart-felt cry?

See how your wealth could speed God's Word,
This is your privileged part,
But comfort is to be preferred –
How empty is your heart!

Ah, you are seen! God's piercing eye
An awful sight reveals;
Repulsive selfishness puffed high
That dignity conceals.

Oh, come to Calvary and die
To hidden carnal pride!
Where self-indulgent cravings lie,
And earthly values guide.

Then yield to Him your treasured gain,
Self-seeking crucified,
'Twill gather fields of ripened grain,
True riches multiplied.

Whom Shall I Send?

Tune: (**8886** with refrain) **S. of V. 714** or Tongue can tell (*The love that Jesus had for me...*) Redemption Songs 126 or Misericordia S.ofV.628a – Saffron Walden 628b
Drawn to the cross
or Woodworth S.ofV. 339 M.P. 396(i) *Just as I am*

"Also I heard the voice of the Lord, saying, Whom shall I send, and who will go for us? Then said I, Here am I, send me."
Is. 6:8

"Whom shall I send?" the prophet heard
When he, enraptured, saw the Lord;
He rose and went, his spirit stirred,
"Whom shall I send today?"

Whom shall I send? Oh hear the cry!
Whom shall I send? From sky to sky!
Whom shall I send to bring men nigh?
Whom shall I send today?

Do the bright youth no longer care?
Do they not see the treasures rare?
Where are they then, oh where, oh where?
Whom shall I send today?

Following far they hear no call!
Sleeping so sound while millions fall!
Do they not care at all – at all?
Whom shall I send today?

Whom shall I send? Oh who will go?
Who then will preach with a voice of woe?
Who will be sped by love's strong bow?
May I send YOU today?

Lord of the harvest; here am I,
I can no more resist Thy cry –
Cost what it may, to live or die,
Send me, dear Lord, today.

I Must

Tune: *(10 10 10 10)* Woodlands S.ofV.76b M.P.631 (ii) *Tell out my soul*
or Morecambe S.ofV.555 *My goal is God Himself*
or Yanworth S.ofV.679,M.P.178 *Go forth and tell*

*"And other sheep I have, which are not of this fold: them also **I must** bring,
and they shall hear my voice; and there shall be one fold, and one shepherd."*
John 10:16

I must about my Father's business be,
Must work the works of Him who now sends Me,
Fulfil His will by love's extremity –
I cannot stay! I must go forth! I must!

I must my Father's sacred will now do,
Must preach in Galilean cities too,
My other sheep, them also I must woo –
I cannot stay! I must go forth! I must!

Constrained, compelled by Love's Almighty flow,
Like flint My face set to the awful woe,
My inmost soul consumed by Love – I go!
I cannot stay! I must go forth! I must!

The glory which shall follow I behold,
The million, million souls, more bright than gold,
The Lamb be slain and then there be one fold!
I cannot stay! I must go forth! I must!

O soul, and do you claim that He is thine,
When worldly and self-centred you recline?
When sacrificial service you decline?
You do not go, nor can you say, "I must."

O God, the bonds that bind us – strong unseen!
Deliver Lord, set free and make us clean,
Oh, crucify in us the low and mean!
That we may hear the words of Christ, "I must!"

Then fill with burning Love so mightily,
That we will go compelled by Calvary,
And one in passion, one, O Christ, with Thee,
Will cry with joy, "I must go forth! I must!"

Tunes

which can be used for many of the poems

	Songs of Victory	Mission Praise	Title

CM (Common Metre)

	Songs of Victory	Mission Praise	Title
Abney	170		Alas and did my Saviour bleed
Abridge	411	31	O Jesus Christ, grow Thou in me
Gerontius	39	563	Praise to the Holiest in the height.
Glasgow	221		Behold! the mountain of the Lord
Kedron	307		Come, let us to the Lord
Lloyd	97c		How sweet the name of Jesus sounds
Martyrdom	556		Oh for a closer walk with God
Saltzburg	435		O God of Bethel
Sawley	600		Oh for a heart to praise my God
St. Agnes, Durham	503		Jesus the very thought of Thee
St. Anne	70	498	O God our help in ages past
St. Columba	247		Come Holy Ghost our hearts inspire
St. Magnus	218b	647	The head that once was crowned
St. Peter	97a	251	How sweet the name of Jesus sounds
St. Saviour	197	210	Hark the glad sound the Saviour comes
St.Stephen (Abridge)	601		Oh for a heart to praise my God
St. Stephen (Newington)	592	329	Lord I believe a rest remains
Stracathro	543	328	Approach my soul, the mercy seat
Westminster	30	468	My God how wonderful Thou art

Metrical Psalms
(All metrical psalms are **CM**)

	Songs of Victory	Mission Praise	Title
Stroudwater	57		God is our refuge and our strength
St Magnus Nottingham	72	647	O sing a new song
Ballerma	372		I waited for the Lord my God
Bays of Harris	550b		
Belmont	252		Thy word is to my feet a lamp
Coleshill	33		O thou my soul, bless God the Lord
Crimmond	438b	660	The Lord's my shepherd
Creator God	464	583	Safe in the shadow of the Lord
Effingham	62		His Name for ever shall endure
French	428		I to the hills will lift mine eyes
Irish	69		O come let us sing
Jackson	251	323	That man that hath perfect blessedness
Orlington	438a		The Lord's my shepherd

LM (long metre)

	Songs of Victory	Mission Praise	Title
Brookfield	499	346	It is a thing most wonderful
Church Triumphant	219	761	The Lord is King
Deep Harmony	533	620	Sweet is the work
Duke Street	106a	143	Jesus shall reign
Fulda	523	728	Lord Jesus Christ, we seek Thy face
Grateful Praise	31		Now in a song of grateful praise
Hereford	699b		O Thou who camest from above
Holly	694b		Lord speak to me
Maryton	63	383	Lord of all being throned afar
Old Hundredth	42	20	Praise God from whom all blessings flow

	Songs of Victory	Mission Praise	Title
Ombersley	686	250	How shall they hear?
Pentecost	234		O Spirit of the living God
Retreat	518		From every stormy wind that blows
Rimington	106b	171	Jesus shall reign
Rockingham	195a	755	When I survey the wondrous cross
(Scottish Melody)	195b		When I survey the wondrous cross
Truro	253	379	Arm of the Lord
Warrington	196	738	We sing the praise
Whitburn	694a	444	Lord speak to me